Sojourners of Truth and Justice:
Voices in Black and White...

Sojourners of Truth and Justice: Voices in Black and White...

A TRIBUTE

Augustella Clay

To order additional copies of this book, contact:
Xlibris Corporation
1-888-795-4274
www.Xlibris.com

61256

Contents

DEDICATED TO THE . . .

Memory of the eight individuals to whom this tribute is paid and to each one of us—citizens in this life sojourn . . . their legacies:

SOJOURNER TRUTH AND SUSAN B. ANTHONY
Parallel voices in the advocacy for women's rights
ELEANOR ROOSEVELT AND MARY MC LEOD BETHUNE
Parallel voices for Human rights, Civil rights and justice
ED BRADLEY AND WALTER CRONKITE
Parallel voices in Journalistic integrity, sensitivity, and truth
ANN RICHARDS AND BARBARA JORDAN
Parallel voices in Political eloquence and Equity

And, as always:
To my husband Jim; to 'favorite son,' Jason; and 'favorite daughter,'
Erika, with gratitude and humility for your loving support.

Preface

Our desire is to pay tribute to each of the aforementioned individuals who seem connected to one another by a tapestry of intricate common threads crossing cultural, gender, and generational lines. From our vantage point, they represent prime examples, verbal portraits of people who modeled their passion. They each were humble in character, great in the honesty utilized in exercising their craft. Each sojourn, literal and figurative, enabled them to travel miles of tension, wrestling, searching, struggle and revelation before they transitioned.

Each one of them leaves indelible imprints, etched permanently within the annals of time that from our perspective should not go unnoticed. They not only talked the talk of their sojourn with voices that resonate with passion and universality; they walked the walk with eloquence truth and justice. They exemplified seminal leadership, innovation, proactivity, trustworthiness, tolerance, humility and unity in their diversity.

Wearing well the traveling shoes of their life mission, their sojourn continues in their legacies. We don't believe that anyone of them set out to be a hero or heroine, a 'she-roe' or 'sheroine' (author's adaptation). We do believe that those great attributes were their destiny and that they willingly yielded to those ordained roles chosen for each of them by life itself.

Our search took us to biographies; eulogies; free encyclopedia references; personal and vicarious reflections as resonating voices seen, heard, and witnessed by the testimony of others. We pondered notes from public record archives made available as permanent 'her-stories' and 'histories.' The result is this, a different periscope, 'fusion narratives,' of the lives of these unique individuals setting the stage for new beginnings as viable starting points for more in-depth explorations into a plethora of other possibilities, perched on the ledge of the near and distant future.

Glossary

Justice: Fair, truthful, uncompromising treatment

Sojourner: Traveler, one on a journey, mission, a wanderer, a searcher, a seeker

Truth: Proven, without question, not false, accurate, valid, reliable, absolute; information agreed upon by recognized experts as having relevance and being without error or flaw and rightly interpreted

Voice: Speaker, verbal picture, metaphor for the actual person, viewpoint, passion

Acknowledgments

Heartfelt thanks to those of you who provided your input to this book by sharing your views to the 'conversation' regarding the individuals being recognized herein for their extraordinary contributions to this 'fusion' life sojourn. We've heard it said that "One picture is worth a thousand words." (Unknown source) And, conversely, these verbal narratives, are the 'thousand words' the canvas upon which the pictures and portraits that depict the honorees recognized in this book, are based.

Dr. John C. Raines, of Temple University (Philadelphia, PA), in his book: *The Justice Men Owe Women* notes " . . . Every book is part of a conversation. It is borne out of conversation and returns itself to that conversation." (xiii) Consequently, we recognize and celebrate your 'voice' shared in this another phase of the on-going dialogue within a conversation.

Does it Make a Difference?

Reprinted from The Spirit of Beauty He Holds the Reins by permission of the author Augustella Clay

It matters not in the clasping of hands,
whether the right hand covers the left or the left hand
covers the right
As long as the clasp is firm and true.
What difference does it make if
when walking one traverses
This land putting the right foot
before the left
As long as one stands tall and walks with
dignity and purpose?
It matters not the hue of our fleshly outer garment
for we are all created in God's image.
What difference does it make when one
completes a task, what tune they marched to as long as
long as one was in tune with oneself
and the task was approached with an attitude
of deliverance? The persistent pursuit was
as human gadflies-piercing, probing and pricking
consciences until they were noticed, heard, and responded to
with voices in dialogue. And, action taken to
correct the injustice.
What difference does it make if one is unique in giving
the very best that they are capable of giving
to this life journey?
The only difference is one that really makes a difference!

Quotations

"If the first woman God ever made was strong enough to turn the world upside down all alone, these women together ought to be able to turn it back and get it right-side up again. And now that they are asking to do it, the men better let them."

Sojourner Truth
"I speak the truth about injustice."

Sojourner Truth
"Truth is powerful and it prevails."

Sojourner Truth
"The Spirit calls me, and I must go."
(After changing her name and traveling as an itinerant preacher)

Sojourner Truth
"I have plowed and reaped and husked and chopped and mowed, and can any man do more than that?

Sojourner Truth
"I am not going to die, I'm going home like a shooting star."

Sojourner Truth
"I shall earnestly and persistently continue to urge all women to the practical recognition of the old Revolutionary maxim. Resistance to tyranny is obedience to God."

Susan B. Anthony

"Cautious, careful people, always casting about to preserve their reputations . . . can never effect a reform."
Susan B. Anthony

"I beg you to speak of Woman as you do of the Negro, speak to her as a human being, as a citizen of the United States, as a half of the people in whose hands lies the destiny of this Nation."
Susan B. Anthony

"Organize, agitate, educate, must be our war cry."
Susan B. Anthony

CHAPTER *1*

SOJOURNER TRUTH

NOVEMBER 18, 1797-NOVEMBER 26, 1883

SUSAN B. ANTHONY

FEBRUARY 15, 1820-MARCH 13, 1906

Parallel voices in advocacy for women's rights

Sojourner Truth and Susan B. Anthony, along with so many dedicated others, contributed greatly to the women's struggle for rights. They were tireless social activists who worked to achieve justice and fully human citizenship in both the public and private spheres for women. Although one woman was a medium built, plain, white, single woman, with sharp facial features, who never married; and the other a towering, comely, black woman, former slave who possessed a powerful speaking voice and equally melodious singing voice, who sang Spirituals that calmed the savage breasts who came to hear her speak; they were connected. Their lives were parallel as their voices converged in the musical, harmonious liner notes, spaces, crescendos, rests, and allegro movements of 'her-story.' They were compatible 'dancers' in the unified, rhythmic goal of truth, justice and human rights.

Sojourner Truth was an enigma. How was it possible for a woman who could neither read nor write, labeled 'illiterate' speak with such power and persuasion? Did she receive power from the Word, the foundation of her religious belief? Only her God knows for sure the answer to that query. Only her God knows the how and why underlying the 'TRUTH' in her being as a living, breathing, 'power house.' Her mission so passionately stated, was to advocate for women's rights, women's equity, and women's suffrage and religious salvation. She sought equal treatment and justice, as a human first, with dignity and worth; and as a first class citizen. Her stated role was to 'walk the roads of life, work against injustice, and speak the truth.' (Authors paraphrase)

Accounts of Sojourner Truth's powerful oratory indicate that she was 'mesmerizing' in effect. So when this towering woman raised up her 6 foot—plus torso on stage and approached the podium to speak, though plain of face, unsophisticated and basic in grammar and syntax, she was transformed into a 'lioness;' as a lioness with a cause and the 'roar' emitting from her mouth, she was a definite force to be reckoned with. In my mind's eye and with the ears of my spirit I can hear and see the 'spiritual testimony of this giant of a woman with a cause, a woman on a mission. 'I'm on my journey now, and I walks' the world and I speaks the truth, and 'ain't' I a woman?' As she proceeded with that renowned speech, the signature statement of her sojourn, the heckler's stopped heckling; the nay Sayers ceased their negativity. Boos' were converted to cheers, the antagonists became advocates and the dissonant audience became at one with the dynamic speaker. The fragments of the potential mob became a captive audience, attentive and unified.

No narrative entitled 'Sojourners of Truth' would be complete without recognizing the woman who adopted the name Sojourner Truth. She was born into slavery in Ulster County, New York sometime between the late 1700's and early 1800's. Although the exact date of her birth is unknown, it is often documented as 1797. Her parents James and Betsey named her Isabella Baumbree. They were slaves of a 'Low' Dutch family called Ardinburgh. Forced into marriage, at age fourteen, with an older slave called Thomas who was also owned by their slave holder, at that time. His name was John Dumont. Elizabeth and Thomas had four children between the years 1815 and 1826. Their names were: Diana, Peter, Elizabeth and Sophia. Isabella suffered greatly most of her life since her freedom was usurped at birth and she lived through subsequent unheard of, inhumane atrocities to her person. She told of daily physical, emotional, and sexual abuse at the hands of both male and female slave owners. She reported that she had been beaten, lacerated, raped, bound and tortured, seemingly because she was alive, in those places, and a female.

Isabella changed her name, upon gaining her freedom, at age 43, to Sojourner Truth. Once set free, she proclaimed to fulfill her mission ordained by God. Religion lay at the foundation of her profound change from a victim enslaved, to a survivor with unique charismatic leadership abilities. Ironically too, English was her second language. Dutch was her first. The rest of this story is well documented history or better yet 'her-story', and a matter of public record.

The researchers tell us that her grandson, Sammy Banks, became an integral part or her entourage. He traveled with her and served as her literary agent to perform any tasks requiring reading for clarity and writing. He was only twenty-four years old at his untimely death, in 1875. Sojourner Truth became one of the best-known and well-revered social activists, champion of justice, truth, and the rights of women.

Sojourner Truth was one of the new faces attending the 1850 first National Women's Rights Convention, in Worcester, Mass. This convention patterned after the seminal visionary meetings at Seneca Falls, New York, in 1848, which demanded women being accorded the same rights afforded men. Charismatic with a unique sense of humor candor and wit, she encountered the likes of Harriet Tubman and Elizabeth Cady Stanton, Harriet Beecher Stowe, Lucretia Mott, and Susan B. Anthony.

She was invited to the White House on three separate occasions, to meet with President Abraham Lincoln regarding the abolition of slavery, women's suffrage and human rights. During her first visit with President Lincoln, Ms Truth shared with him the fact that prior to his run for the President, she had never heard of him. He in turn informed her that her reputation had preceded her. He shared with her the fact that she was, indeed known to him. In the notes that Truth dictated to a friend, after her first visit with Lincoln, she remarked about his grace and respect shown to her. He invited her back to the White House for a second visit. From all indications, Truth viewed the President as a new friend. He even provided her with a personal autograph for a book that she had in her possession at the time of her visit. Although I found no record to indicate that Lincoln and Truth were related to each other in any way, he signed her book:

"For Aunty Sojourner Truth, A. Lincoln, October29, 1864."

Her comments related to this event indicate that she was enthralled by the fact that "the same hand that signed the Emancipation Proclamation to free the slaves, with the same hand that signed the death-warrant of slavery . . ." he signed her book. (Butler, Mary G., *The Words of Truth*, Heritage Battle Creek, A Journal of Local History. Vol 8, Fall 1997.)

She was a sought after speaker by many religious and social organizations throughout the country. Her involvements were with predominantly white communes, Methodists, Quakers, and abolitionist organizations. With a powerful voice of authority and compassion, she spoke for prison reform, temperance, and the rights of freedmen. She lobbied the federal government to assist the freedmen with relocation costs, land, and transportation to new homes in western states such as Kansas. She waged legal battles on behalf of human rights and successfully won three of those law suits brought against the establishment. One successful legal battle won involved the freeing of her own son who was being held illegally.

Truth also met with another President, President Ulysses S. Grant, to advocate the rights of women. It remains a 'mystery' as to how this woman remembered for her stellar oratory, captivating songs, communicator with Presidents, respected and admired for her ability to comprehend, analyze and deliver eloquent speeches, was, even to the time of her death, considered 'illiterate.' Others have documented the oral history she shared regarding the cruelties she endured. Yet, she was a survivor and overcame obstacles to become a homeowner and a sought after speaker on the lecture tour. An advocate for the dispossessed, she was passionate and fearless in her efforts. Her sharp mind, shrewd judgment, keen sense of humor and powerful presence gained her much respect.

A resourceful person, Sojourner, though a 'plain woman,' in appearance, who enjoyed wearing the simple Quaker garb, supported herself by selling her portraits. She captioned the portraits: "I sell the Shadow to support the Substance." (Mary G. Butler, for the Sojourner Truth Institute of Battle Creek in association with the Historical Society of Battle Creek.) Sojourner first came to Michigan, in 1856 when she was invited to address an Association meeting of the Friends of Human Progress. A year later she returned to a settlement in Michigan called Harmonia and bought a home there. In 1867 she moved to the city of Battle Creek, bought another home and remained there until her death in 1883.

Susan B. Anthony (February 15, 1820-March 13, 1906) was befriended by Sojourner Truth. Prior to their association, however, Anthony's collaboration and friendship with another women's advocate, Elizabeth Cady Stanton is well documented. Cady Stanton is noted for convening, along with four other women activists, the first Women's Rights Convention in Seneca Falls New York in July, 1848. Of great significance, at this convention attended by more than three hundred women and men, was the drafting and adoption of a *Declaration of Sentiments,* in which the women documented their demands for women to receive the same rights accorded to men in the *Declaration of Independence.* The women used it as a blueprint to justify their resolutions and to motivate the audience to support and commit to their demands for equal treatment under the law, women's rights to speak in public, *voting rights,* equal education, access to professions and trades; rights to make contracts, own property, testify in court, have guardianship over children, as well as equality in marriage.

Two years later in October 1850, Sojourner Truth, and Harriet Tubman (General Moses of underground railroad notoriety), were new faces in attendance , attracted to the first National Women's Rights Convention held in Worcester, Massachusetts. In the spring of 1851, Sojourner Truth was invited to speak at the gathering of women's rights activists, in Akron, Ohio. This was the occasion for the initiation of her famous signature speech *". . . and ain't I a woman," provoked by a male clergy heckler who mocked women* for, in his opinion, being unable to handle the responsibility and trust required and necessary for them to exercise their vote, because of physical weakness. Truth is purported to have said: *"The man over there says women need to be helped into carriages and lifted over ditches, and to have the best place everywhere. Nobody ever helps me into carriages or over puddles, or gives me the best place—and ain't I a woman?"*

Susan B. Anthony was formally introduced into the women's rights movement in 1852, when she attended the third national convention with the largest documented delegates in attendance of two thousand participants. Susan B. Anthony, by this time had overcome her early reluctance for public speaking. As she gained more confidence in her passion for the egalitarian treatment of women, she became more knowledgeable regarding the advocacy for women's rights. Thus, it seems natural for her to accept an invitation to speak at the third annual Women's Rights Convention in Syracuse in 1852. As a stirring new voice for change in the way the society and government treated women in the United States, she availed herself of this opportunity to present her first speech at the convention. Her more than half—century friendship with Elizabeth Cady Stanton began the year before. Anthony met Stanton in 1851. They were introduced to each other by a mutual friend during a chance meeting on the street in Seneca Falls. Subsequent to that chance meeting, Anthony and Stanton traveled extensively throughout the United States speaking on women's rights. Other prominent and notable names as warriors for women's rights included: Mary Ann McClintock, Jane Hurt, Lucretia Mott, Martha Wright, and Harriet Beecher Stowe, writer for the Atlantic Monthly, who referred to Truth as a *"Libyan Sibyl."*

Anthony and Stanton published their first weekly journal, in New York. It was called *The Revolution. The motto for the publication was: "The true republic-men, their rights and nothing more; women their rights and nothing less."* Anthony served as the business manager for the magazine and Stanton served as the editor. The main issues addressed in the publication included the rights of all women, including African-American women, to vote, it also discussed pay equity issues, sought to promote more liberal divorce laws and sought to address the church's position on women's issues. The magazine was underwritten independently by philanthropist George Francis Train, who provided them with $600 as start-up funds. Although she never married, this did not serve as a deterrent to Anthony who wrote freely regarding her views on sexuality in marriage and a woman's rights and control over her own body. Anthony seemed to exhibit some of the progressive-mindedness displayed by her own mother. She spoke and seemed to discern the relevancy of issues regarding human rights well in advance of the time and culture in which she lived. These same issues addressed as relevant in the 19th and 20th century, are still major areas of concern in the present 21st century.

Men were also well represented at the varied Women's Conventions and influential in the drafting and adoption of the 'Declaration of Sentiments and Resolutions' for equal treatment of women. Abolitionist Frederick Douglass was a prominent voice and highly visible participant. He and Susan B. Anthony became friends. The Convention mantra of vision with purpose followed by action was designed to ignite momentum and energy for feminist activism and women's equity. In 1869 for the first time during the course of their long-time association and friendship, Anthony and Douglass found themselves diametrically opposed to one another regarding the debate regarding the 15th Amendment to the Constitution. It was thought that the Amendment initially was directed towards granting both male and female blacks suffrage. The American Equal Rights Association (AERA) voted to support the Amendment on that basis. In actuality it was discovered that the 15th Amendment to the Constitution was designed to grant voting rights to black men and not to women. The disagreement between Anthony and Douglass ensued when she questioned why women, who were members of AERA, should support the 15th Amendment while Douglass and his male colleagues seemed hesitant to encourage black men to also continue to fight for voting rights for women.

Susan B. Anthony was unstoppable in her determination to attain the vote for women and her advocacy for equity for women as citizens of inclusion. She was arrested on November 18, 1872, by a U. S. Deputy Marshall, because she challenged the interpretation of the 14th Amendment and was accused of 'voting illegally in the 1872 Presidential Election, two weeks earlier. In a letter written by Anthony to Stanton, she admitted that she had *"positively voted the Republican ticket-straight . . ." Seven months later, Anthony was tried, convicted and sentenced to pay a fine, but not imprisonment. She said in court that she did not intend to ever pay that penalty imposed upon her for her alleged crime of voting. She was true to her word and even up to her dying day the fine had never been paid.* Her argument regarding the interpretation of the 14th Amendment was that it guaranteed *"to all persons born or naturalized in the United States"* the privileges of citizenship, and since it did not include verbiage excluding anyone by 'gender qualification' this gave women the constitutional right to vote in federal elections, by default. The trial served as a vehicle for Susan B. Anthony to spread her arguments to a wider audience than anticipated or imagined.

Anthony was the first woman to have her image imprinted on the currency of the USA, the silver dollar. Although the gesture was admirable, one is forced to question the rationale behind making the coin so small that it was often mistaken for a quarter then in circulation which reduced its value to only ¼ of its true value of the silver dollar. Was this just a mere oversight or was this a blatant insult to the feminist movement in general and to Susan B. Anthony, specifically??? Was this gesture a mere patriarchal 'faux pas' or a deliberate insult and act of indifference? Why not create a coin of equal size, since it was expected to be of equal value?

Researchers note that as circulating United States coinage, the Susan B. Anthony dollar was minted only four years (1979, 1980, 1981, and 1999). The coins were produced at the San Francisco mint for the first three production years. They were produced all four years at both the Philadelphia and Denver Mints. The Anthony legacy also documents that her childhood home in Battenville, New York, was placed on the New York Historic Register, in 2006 and on the National Historic Register in 2007. Her home in Rochester, New York, was operated as a museum, after being declared a National Historic Landmark in 1966.

Susan Brownell Anthony died fourteen years, five months, and five days before the passage of the nineteenth amendment (1920), giving women the right to vote. She was the second oldest of seven children born to Daniel Anthony, a cotton manufacturer and abolitionist, and her mother Lucy, a progressive-minded homemaker who had been one of Daniel's former students. Two weeks after the historic Seneca Falls Convention, Lucy attended a women's rights convention at Rochester (1948), and signed her name to the convention's Declaration of Sentiments. They practiced the Quaker religion and maintained a Quaker household (Society of Friends). Daniel did not allow the children to have toys or any other items of amusements with potential for distracting from the "inner light" of their souls. They both believed strongly in one's own self worth. Holding principled convictions, they enforced self-discipline within their family unit. Lucy and Daniel Anthony raised their family in West Grove Massachusetts, near a community called Adams. Their children were born as follows: Guelma Penn (1818), Susan Brownell (1820), Hannah E. (1821), Daniel Read (1824), Mary Stafford (1827), Eliza Tefft (1832) and Jacob Merritt (1834). Daniel Read became active in Kansas in the anti-slavery movement there. Mary Stafford became a teacher and active in the woman's rights movement. Susan B. maintained a close relationship with her sisters throughout her entire active and eventful life.

Commemorative postage stamps have been issued in honor of both Sojourner Truth (February 5, 1986, New Paltz, New York, at the Library named in her honor and Susan B. Anthony (1936 and 1954) Just as Sojourner Truth adopted Battle Creek, Michigan as her new home, they in turn adopted her as daughter, sister, mother, friend, role model, and leader of faith. She was installed in the Seneca Falls, New York, National Women's Hall of Fame, in 1981, and awarded for her achievement in humanitarianism and social progress. She was installed into the Michigan Women's Hall of Fame in 1983. To honor and mark the 200th anniversary of Sojourner's birth, in 1997, Michigan held a year-long celebration, culminating in a national Women's conference and a collectors' commemorative edition of *Heritage Battle Creek* magazine. These great honors recognizing her achievements attained *cosmic proportions,* biographer scholars documented the fact that Sojourner Truth gained *'interplanetary acclaim' because the Mars Pathfinder Microver was named for her.* Renowned Truth biographer, and Princeton professor, Dr. Nell Painter, in her book, *Painter, Sojourner Truth: A Life, A Symbol, wrote: "Empowered by her religious faith, the former slave worked tirelessly for many years to transform national attitudes and institutions. No other woman who had gone through the ordeal of slavery managed to survive with sufficient strength, poise and self—confidence to become a public presence over the long term." (4)*

In May, 2009, as a tribute to the memory of Sojourner Truth and her tireless work as a pioneer for truth and proponent of justice, was the unveiling of a statue of this dedicated leader, in the nation's Capitol by First Lady of the United States of America, Michelle Obama, wife of the 44th President, Barrack Obama. Others in attendance at the dedication and unveiling of the Sojourner Truth bust were: Nancy Pelosi, Speaker of the House of Representatives; Hilary Rodham Clinton, Secretary of State; and Representative Sheila Jackson Lee, Texas. The bust of Truth is the first one of an African-American to be placed and displayed in the Emancipation Hall along with others recognized as distinguished sojourners of note. Susan B. Anthony along with Elizabeth Cady Stanton and Lucretia Mott, are represented in the United States Capitol, in a sculpture entitled *The Woman Movement,* created by sculptor, Adelaide Johnson. That piece was unveiled in 1921.

Although the lives of Susan B. Anthony and Sojourner Truth were closely intertwined by their passion and values, their differences in stature, flesh tones, age and upbringing made little difference in their overall mission, of equity, unity and overcoming injustice. Thanks to their tireless efforts the 19th Amendment to the Constitution was finally passed, Women's Suffrage means that every woman of voting age has the right to vote. Their legacy continues into the twenty first century in such organizations as The American Association of University Women, (AAUW) the National Organization of Women (NOW), and the League of Women Voters, just to name a few.

Quotations

"Of one thing I am sure, in order to be useful we must stand for the things we feel are right, and we must work for those things wherever we find ourselves. It does very little good to believe in something unless you tell your friends and associates about your beliefs."

Eleanor Roosevelt

"The world over, people are considering the radio more and more a necessity. They listen when they would not read, perhaps some of them cannot read. If we could get in the habit of sending important messages which represent the thinking of groups of people throughout the world, from one nation to another, I feel sure it would increase our knowledge and understanding of each other."

Eleanor Roosevelt
April 10, 1939

"Proof to the world that a government is stable and strong lies in the ability of its leaders to show their lack of fear by their generosity to the opposition. Too many people today seem to think that strength lies only in cruelty and force. Temporarily this may be true, but it can never win out in the end."

Eleanor Roosevelt
April 3, 1939

"When you love people very much, isn't it grand to be able to join in their happiness? Like everything else in the world, however, there is a price to pay for love, for the more happiness we derive from the existence and companionship of other human beings, the more vulnerable we are when there is any cause for apprehension. It takes courage to love, but pain through love is the purifying fire which those who live generously know.

We all know people who are so much afraid of pain that they shut themselves up like clams in a shell and, giving out nothing, receive nothing and therefore shrink until life is a mere living death."

Eleanor Roosevelt
April 1, 1939

Source: My Day by Eleanor Roosevelt United Feature Syndicate, Inc.

Quotations

"Next to God we are indebted to women, first for life itself, and then for making it worth living."

Mary McLeod Bethune

"Knowledge is the prime need of the hour."

Mary McLeod Bethune

"Invest in the human soul. Who knows, it might be a diamond in the rough."

Mary McLeod Bethune

"If we accept and acquiesce in the face of discrimination, we accept the responsibility ourselves and allow those responsible to salve their conscience by believing that they have our acceptance and concurrence. We should, therefore, protest openly everything . . . that smacks of discrimination or slander."

Mary McLeod Bethune

CHAPTER 2

ELEANOR ROOSEVELT

OCTOBER 11, 1884 – NOVEMBER 7, 1962

MARY MC LEOD BETHUNE

JULY 10, 1875 – MAY 18, 1955

Parallel voices for Human rights, Civil rights and Justice

Both Eleanor Roosevelt and Mary McLeod Bethune were adamant in their passion for egalitarian and just treatment of all human beings. They shared an advocacy for *speaking the truth to power*. They both became educators and worked tirelessly in social service efforts with concerns for promoting social welfare and assuring basic human rights to people individually and collectively.

The women first met in the 1920's at a luncheon hosted by Mrs. Roosevelt's Mother –in-law. When a life of privilege converged with a life of humble circumstances, the results melded into productive efforts to empower others. They became friends and spent the rest of their parallel lives engaged in humanitarian endeavors. When they identified a particular need, they expended extraordinary efforts to meet that need through their own efforts and through the efforts of others whom they were able to influence and solicit. Their mantra was equality, inclusion, unity in diversity, and the pursuit of fulfilled lives, liberty and happiness for all those under the banner of . . ."we the people."Each one helped the other to advance a wide range of social service and political causes.

Because of her highly visible friendship, relationship, and association with Mrs. Roosevelt and then President Franklin Delano Roosevelt and his 'New Deal' government, Mary McLeod Bethune was appointed to lead and coordinate numerous projects and committees in the fight for racial equality. She was afforded the opportunity to serve, informally as the federal administrations 'race leader at large.' She served in this capacity from 1936 to 1943. Her role in the organization of the Federal Council on Negro Affairs AKA the Black Cabinet thrust her into the prominent position of being the highest ranking black woman in government at that point in time. (Appiah, Gates, *Africana*, 230, 1999)

Additional *parallels* shared by Mary McLeod Bethune and Eleanor Roosevelt centered around their roles in marriages that required each one to step-up and to step-out into their *sojourns*, respectively into roads less traveled by. Married to Albertus Bethune, in 1898, they became the parents of one child, a son Albert. The marriage did not last and they were separated because Mr. Bethune did not share her views, dedication and commitment involving the uplifting, educating, and service to the down trodden and marginalized.

Mrs. Roosevelt was 'separated' too in a sense, by the polio which limited the mobility of her husband. As a team, Roosevelt and Bethune broke through many barriers. As human rights advocates, *united in their diversity* they shared gender, generation, and national culture.

Born into poverty, July 10, 1875 in Mayesville, South Carolina, the fifteenth of seventeen offspring of parents who were former slaves; Mary McLeod Bethune became an educator. She founded the National Council of Negro Women, in 1935, and served as its first president. She was a director of The National Youth Administration from 1936 to 1944. Mrs. Bethune died of a heart attack in 1955. Her home in Washington, D.C. Is a national historic site, open to visitors on a routine basis. Her numerous awards and honors for her notable achievements in women's rights and civil rights, included the prestigious Spingarn Medal, awarded to her in 1935, by the National Association For the Advancement of Colored People (NAACP).

Eleanor Roosevelt was raised by her grandmother, in Tivoli, New York, after the death of both her parents. Her mother died in 1892, and her father died two years later.

Raised as a child of privilege, she was educated by tutors, privately, until the age of fifteen. She was then sent to a girl's school in England where she remained until she reached age 18. Her thinking and education were greatly influenced by the headmistress, at the school, Mademoiselle Marie Souvestre, who placed great emphasis on social service and charitable humanitarian concerns.

Eleanor Roosevelt or ER as she became known for her signature sign-off to her newspaper column, *My Day, which appeared six-days a week between 1935 and 1962 c*hose to share her daily activities with as many readers as possible. Her writings were presented as journal entries since she did not keep a personal diary.

United in marriage to Franklin Delano Roosevelt, her fifth cousin, in March 17, 1905, that union produced six offspring between the years 1906 and 1916. Their names in order were: Franklin Delano, Jr., Anna Eleanor; John; Franklin Delano Jr.; Elliott, and James. The scope of her public service activities broadened to include issues related to her husbands' political career goals as well as her own political interests. In 1921, after the president was stricken with polio, Mrs. Roosevelt increased her participation in the political arena as the spokesperson, eyes, ears, limbs and presence of FDR.

Mrs. Roosevelt's numerous public service activities included volunteer work for the American Red Cross, in Navy hospitals, during World War I; the Women's Trade Union League; the League of Women Voters; help in founding a non-profit furniture factory (Val-Kill Industries); and education as a teacher at a private girls' school in New York City. Not only was she able to dispel myths regarding the ability, innate inferiority fallacies, etc. regarding the Tuskegee Airmen. She demonstrated a vote of confidence in their credibility and superior capabilities. Her vote of confidence resulted in Tuskegee Institute being selected as the training site for black officers and pilots in the United States Army Air Corps. On July 23, 1941 Tuskegee Army Airfield was established officially. The pilots, who trained there, were all young and African American. They became part of the 99th and 100th Fighter Squadrons and attained a distinguished, proven, military track record. They are noted for successfully rescuing members of the armed services when completing their varied hazardous wartime combat missions overseas, during World War II. They never lost a troop, group, squadron, or cargo. On her own volition, Eleanor Roosevelt elected to be flown by a crew of Tuskegee Airmen as a representative of President FDR, thereby fulfilling a dual role . . . his and her own as a whole person sojourner; a woman of dignity and worth. In her own way she illustrated genuine respect, tolerance, and acceptance of others. Her action on April 19, 1941, was the impetus to establish the Tuskegee Airmen program. She posed a question to African American pilot Charles "Chief" Anderson, at Moton Field, in Tuskegee, Alabama she asked him: "Can Negroes really fly airplanes?" On that eventful day "Chief" Anderson took controls as pilot of a Piper J-3 Cub, and took Mrs. Roosevelt on a short flight. And, as noted above, the rest is history and "her-story." Her lifelong work involved advocacy of the needs and rights of the disadvantaged, the poor, the disenfranchised, and minorities. She seemed to take pride in proving the antagonists wrong.

Another very telling episode in the life and sojourn of Eleanor Roosevelt was related to her action against racism and on behalf of world-renowned opera singer, Marian Anderson of Philadelphia, Pennsylvania. Preceded by her celebrity, Ms Anderson was invited by the Daughters of the American Revolution (DAR), to sing in concert at its venue Constitution Hall, in Washington, D.C. Apparently in 1932, subsequent to protests from its members and followers over Ms Anderson's race and the potential for mixed-race—seating" at concerts, the DAR had adopted a rule excluding 'mixed seating.' After discovering that Ms Anderson was African-American the DAR rescinded their invitation to her to sing in Constitution Hall; Eleanor

Roosevelt modeled morality and her advocacy of *truth and justice* when she in a notable act of conscience and resistance to racial discrimination, in protest, publicly *resigned* her membership from the DAR. Her subsequent actions resulted in Ms Anderson being invited by the federal government to sing at a public recital on the steps of the Lincoln Memorial. The Washington Mall served as her outdoor auditorium Thus, on April 9, 1939, Easter Sunday, in the radiance of the 'Son's' sun beaming brightly, Marian Anderson was thrust into national and international prominence when she sang a free concert recital to an audience of more than 75,000 people of all races and creeds crowded together to hear her. One of the Spirituals she sang, on that momentous occasion: "Nobody Knows the Trouble I've Seen" and 'America' a national hymn/anthem, seemed to provide a fitting impact for that eventful moment in time.

In 2009, on Easter Sunday, another opera singer and 'daughter' of Philadelphia, Denise Graves, in tribute to Anderson, replicated her stirring performance by including the aforementioned two selections in her recital, which was also performed on the steps of the Lincoln Memorial to a crowd of thousands. The scholars tell us that in 1943 the D.A.R. extended another invitation to Marian Anderson to perform at Constitution Hall for a war relief effort, this time *without rejecting the artist, without exclusion of attendees, and without placing restrictions on 'mixed-seating.'*

Senator Hillary Rodham Clinton, currently Secretary of State in the Obama Administration in the Foreword to Volume 1 of *The Eleanor Roosevelt Papers,* noted that one would be struck by the breadth of the interest, concerns, ideals, honesty, passion, and eloquence revealed in the papers. She wrote that they seemed to translate Ms Roosevelt's life experiences into her significant efforts on behalf of others which greatly embodied the struggles of marginalized people in the early twentieth century. A final note documents the honor bestowed on Eleanor Roosevelt for her " . . . work, her *legacy,* her timeless values and ideals, and her commitment to imagining a better future for all people . . . and the hope that those who read her words will accept and acknowledge them as a 'call to action.'"

The Legacy of Mary McLeod Bethune though unique, in many aspects, closely parallels Eleanor Roosevelt's in that she too hoped that her rich life experiences from which she expended much blood, sweat, sorrow and 'distilled' principles and policies to formulate her philosophy which may be a source of inspiration to future generations. The following is a paraphrase of the Bethune Legacy as documented by the National Council of Negro Women: (I accept this legacy as a call to action and as a personal gift to me and my sister members of NCNW)

"I leave you Love. Love thy neighbor's is a precept which could transform the world if it were universally practiced. Loving your neighbor means being interracial, inter religious, and international.

I leave you hope . . . . Yesterday, our ancestors endured the degradation of slavery, yet they retained their dignity. Today, we direct our economic and political strength toward winning a more abundant and secure life.

I leave you a thirst for education. Knowledge is the prime need of the hour . . . . If we continue in this trend, we will be able to rear increasing numbers of strong purposeful men and women, equipped with vision, mental clarity, health and education.

I leave you the challenge of developing confidence in one another . . . . We must spread out as far and as fast as we can, but we must also help each other as we go.

I leave you a respect for the use of power . . . . It has always been my first concern that this power should be placed on the side of human justice . . . . We must select leaders who are wise and courageous, and of great moral stature and ability . . . . .who will work not for themselves, but for others.

I leave you faith . . . . Without faith nothing is possible. With it, nothing is impossible. Faith in God is the greatest power, but great too is faith in oneself.

I leave you racial dignity . . . . Despite many crushing burdens and handicaps, I have risen from the cotton fields of South Carolina to found a college, administer it during its years of growth, become a public servant in government and country, and a leader of women. I would not exchange my color for all the wealth in the world, for had I been born white, I might not have been able to do all I have done or yet hope to do.

I leave you a desire to live harmoniously with your fellow man . . . . We Must learn to deal with people positively and on an individual basis.

I leave you, finally, a responsibility to our young people. The world around us really belongs to youth . . . . They must not be discouraged from aspiring toward greatness, for they are the leaders of tomorrow. Nor, must they forget that the masses of our people are still underprivileged, ill-housed, impoverished, and victimized by discrimination.

FAITH, COURAGE, BROTHERHOOD, DIGNITY, AMBITION, RESPONSIBILITY-these are needed today as never before . . . . The Freedom Gates are half ajar. We must pry them fully open.

IF I HAVE A LEGACY TO LEAVE MY PEOPLE, IT IS MY PHILOSOPHY OF LIVING AND SERVING. AS I FACE TOMORROW, I AM CONTENT, FOR I THINK I HAVE SPENT MY LIFE WELL. I PRAY NOW THAT MY PHILOSOPHY MAY BE HELPFUL TO THOSE WHO SHARE MY VISION OF A WORLD OF PEACE. The entire Bethune Legacy recognized internationally is inscribed on the base of the Bethune Memorial in Washington, D.C.

The Bethune Memorial is the first of its kind erected (in 1974) in a public park to honor any woman and specifically an African-American woman, Mary McLeod Bethune. It is located in Lincoln Park, a public park in our nation's Capital.

Mary McLeod Bethune founded her first school for girls, in Daytona Beach, Florida: The Daytona Industrial Institute for the Training of Negro Girls with only $1.50 her son, five girl students and her faith in God. During the second year of its existence, the school enrollment grew to one hundred students with three assistant teachers, along with Mrs. Bethune, as faculty. That school evolved into a significant resource within the community and later became the fully accredited, co-educational, Bethune – Cookman College. In 1904 when she needed money to keep the school doors open she baked Sweet Potato pies, fried fish (mullet) made sandwiches and sold them, along with the pies, to workers and others in close proximity to the school. Her Sweet Potato Pies became infamous.

They served as a prime vehicle in helping Mrs. Bethune realize and maintain an entrepreneurial vision, a dream that morphed into the reality it became. Her fund raising efforts were modeled and rivaled only by one, of her 'mentees' and successor, Dr. Dorothy Height. The 'heritage recipe' for those pies is shared by Dr. Dorothy I Height, President/CEO Emeritus National Council of Negro Women, Inc., in *The Black Family Reunion Cookbook (Tradery House 1991)*

Dr. Height also shares this narrative in the book as related to her by Mrs. Bethune: "The Lower 13" was a segregated seating section on a train. It was there that blacks with 'first class tickets' were placed. She also shared with the reader that during these times black women were not addressed with a title of respect. Mature women were often called "Auntie." During one of the many occasions in which Mrs. Bethune was traveling by train, the conductor came to her and addressed her as 'Auntie,' and asked if she could make good biscuits? She replied to him, "I am an advisor to President Roosevelt.

I am the founder of a four year accredited college. I am an organizer of women. I am the organizer and founder of the National Council of Negro Women. I am considered a leader among women. And, I make good biscuits."
(p 40)

Prior to her prominent role in the FDR Administration and her friendship and work related to personal freedom, employment and housing among other notable and significant endeavors, with then 'first-lady' Eleanor Roosevelt, Mrs. Bethune served as advisor at the National Child Welfare Commission, to Presidents Coolidge and Hoover.

Eleanor Roosevelt was a woman of conscience who took appropriate action to illustrate that she seriously "practiced what she preached." Her actions regarding the Tuskegee Airmen is now a matter of public record as is her public support of Marian Anderson and disappointment with her former associates in the DAR for the overt racism they displayed. The latter is evidenced in the resignation letter she wrote to separate herself from the organization. The following text is taken from a copy of the original resignation letter written by Mrs. Roosevelt, as pictured in the National Archives, Still Pictures records, which reads as follows:

Adapted February 28, 1939.

"My dear Mrs. Henry M. Robert: Jr.
I am afraid that I have never been a very
useful member of the Daughters of the
American Revolution, as I know it will
make very little difference to you whether
I resign, or whether I continue to be a
member of your organization.

However, I am in complete disagreement
with the attitude taken in refusing
Constitution Hall to a great artist.
You have set an example which seems to
me unfortunate, and I feel obliged to
send in to you my resignation. You
had an opportunity to lead in an enlightened-
way and it seems to me that your
organization has failed.

I realize that many people will not agree
with me, but feeling as I do this seems
to me the only proper procedure to
follow.

Very sincerely yours, "

From all indications, it appears that Eleanor Roosevelt typed the letter herself with errors left in place to maintain its authenticity. Mrs. Roosevelt was a prolific writer with a plethora of books and articles to her credit. In addition to writing her syndicated column, "My Day," she also wrote for the Ladies Home Journal (1941-49) and Mc Calls Magazine (1949-62).

A sought after lecturer, speaker and public servant, President Truman appointed her to the United Nations (UN) General Assembly United States Delegation. During the drafting of the Universal Declaration of Human Rights, she served as chairperson of the Human Rights Commission. On December 10, 1948, the United Nations General Assembly adopted the declaration drafted under her leadership. In 1953 she served as a volunteer to the American Association for the United Nations Associations. She became an American representative to the World Federation of United Nations Associations. Although the latter work was subsequent to her having resigned from her position to the United States Delegation to the United Nations in 1953, President Kennedy reappointed her to the UN position in 1961 and also appointed her as a member of the Peace Corps National Advisory Committee as well as to the position of chairperson to the President's Commission on the Status of Women.

Mrs. Roosevelt died of apparent natural causes on November 7, 1962, in New York. Mary McLeod Bethune and Eleanor Roosevelt's lives converged in the midst of their passionate missions, seeking, striving, and serving to promote justice, human rights, civil rights, and truth. The steps taken in their sojourn, their respective journeys seemed to focus on those in need, in poverty, downtrodden, those either denied or with limited access to the socio-economic means for securing and maintaining better life, liberty and the pursuit of happiness because of race or gender. They were staunch advocates and proponents of equity. Both women leave legacies of hope, vision, progress, peace and love for humanity.

Quotations

"You know, I think I still have a sense that no matter what you do, no matter what you achieve, no matter how much success you have, no matter how much money you have, relationships are important."

Ed Bradley

"There was no one around me who didn't work hard."

Ed Bradley

"Be prepared, work hard, and hope...."

Ed Bradley

"I knew that God put me on this earth to be on the radio."

Ed Bradley

"Far too often we are judged by the color of our skin and not by the content of our character."

Ed Bradley

"In seeking truth you have to get both sides of a story."

Walter Cronkite

"There is no such thing as a little freedom. Either you are all free, or you are not free."

Walter Cronkite

"Television [is] a high impact medium. It does some things no other force can do-transmitting electronic pictures through the air. Still as an explored, comprehensive medium, it is not a substitute for print."

Walter Cronkite

"When Moses was alive, these pyramids were a thousand years old. Here began the history of Architecture. Here people learned to measure time by a calendar, to plot the stars by astronomy and chart the earth by geometry. And here they developed that most awesome of all ideas-the idea of eternity."

Walter Cronkite

"I can't imagine a person becoming a success who doesn't give this game of life everything he's got."

Walter Cronkite

CHAPTER 3

ED BRADLEY

JUNE 22, 1941-NOVEMBER 9, 2006

WALTER CRONKITE

NOVEMBER 4, 1916-JULY 17, 2009

Parallel voices in Journalistic integrity, sensitivity, and pursuers of truth, Ed Bradley, news correspondent, 60 Minutes on CBS since 1968 and Walter Cronkite, the living legend in his own time, for nineteen years the face of CBS Evening News (starting in 1950.) Each man started out as an ordinary journalist whose work became extraordinary. The 'extra' is the force that makes the difference. Insightful, probing, respectful, prepared, perceptive interviewers, they each were the epitome of *style and* excellence in their craft. Both were well researched. Each one was thorough in preparation with questions designed for the specific guest to elicit truth and in-depth perspective from that specific point of view. The probing verbal pictures that they painted with brush strokes broad enough to enlighten an audience in a balanced, insightful manner, yielded a lasting impression. Seemingly diverse in background, they both became champions in the universality of their missions, their sojourns that made a profound difference in life. As a journalist Bradley never forgot his humble beginnings. Cronkite enjoyed an upper middle-class upbringing, yet he never forgot the trust that the public invested in him to be thorough in maintaining his quest for truth and justice in all his vast, historic, journalistic endeavors, on site or vicariously. Although Bradley and Cronkite will not pass this way again, we hope that their legacies will continue to blaze new trails as advocates of integrity and justice in the journalism 'fourth estate.'

Ed Bradley worked for CBS, '*60 Minutes*'. Cronkite as a pioneer journalist helped to launch CBS News into national and international prominence. Both journalists *were advocates of women and women's rights. Each one took every opportunity opened to them to elevate mentor, coach, or 'pull through the journalistic door,' a female striving and in need of a helping hand or a boost up the ladder of opportunity. They provided support to their male colleagues as well.*

Since our time on earth is limited; it behooves us all to do as much good as we can as often as we can, for as long as we can. 'Todas Tuas' I am all yours. (Latin) seems apropos for the passion both Bradley and Cronkite expended. Men of deep faith, there weren't many of their colleagues who could claim the accolades of besting them in the practice of their craft. They were natural at expressing the core values of this country. Serious journalism was synonymous with each man. Cronkite had a sense of quiet exuberance and excitement. He was a gentleman, an elder statesman of eloquence, a giant among men.

Walter Leland Cronkite, Jr. was born in St. Joseph, Missouri, on November 4, 1916, to his mother Helen, a homemaker, and his father Walter, Sr. a dentist. His grandfather was also a dentist. He was an only child. Since the age of six years old, he expressed a desire to become a newsman. Bringing the Sunday newspaper into the house after its delivery was his first experience handling journalism. The headlines on one fateful day read "Harding Dies."

After his family moved to Houston, Texas, Cronkite took his first foray into journalism by writing for his school newspaper and later working on the yearbook. He attended the University of Texas in 1933 and wrote for the *Daily Texan* while simultaneously working for the *Houston Press,* as a campus correspondent and radio broadcaster. He worked briefly for radio station KNOWS reporting mid-afternoon baseball scores. It seems ironic and certainly not prophetic that one of his administrators at KNOW told him that he would *never* make it in broadcast media. Fortunately, for the world, that fallacious observation did *not* have a 'Pygmalion Effect.' Cronkite's legacy is rich and telling evidence that the KNOW observation was *not* a self-fulfilling prophecy.

At a time when the country had only three broadcast networks, and television was still in its infancy, Walter Cronkite became known as "the most trusted man in America" when he anchored the *CBS Evening News*. Because of his long, on-screen stints, reporting on political conventions and moon launches, he was sometimes dubbed "Old Iron pants." Noted for his in-depth interviews with his high-profile guests, he was recognized for developing a unique and probing approach to elicit truth and clarity from his guests. He sought to personalize his broadcasts for his in studio audience and for the audience at home, concluding with the statement "And, You Were There."

Walter Cronkite lived so much of the history he reported. He interacted with every President from Truman to Obama. On December 7, 1941 Cronkite was working with the United Press International when Pearl Harbor was attacked, thrusting the United States into World War II. While aboard the Battleship Texas, he saw firsthand combat action while the ship was escorting tankers and freighters in the North Atlantic. Several of their caravans were sunk by Nazi warships. In 1943, he was one of six correspondents who flew in a B-17 Flying Fortress with the 8th Air Force during the first bombing runs over Germany. He was aboard another B-17 during the Normandy invasion. Although the plane flew fairly low over Omaha Beach, he was not able to see much action because thick cloud cover blocked out the view.

An anchor of CBS News in 1962, Walter Cronkite had a unique vantage point from which to observe the country's most turbulent times, reporting on the assassination of a President, another destructive war overseas and the eventual resignation of another President. America looked to "Uncle Walter" for unnerving perspective and comfort, for more than half a century. Although his public life fills chronicles of professionalism and avuncular sensitivity, knowledge regarding his personal and private life is limited.

Biographical scholars report that Walter Cronkite was married to Betsy Maxwell Cronkite, in 1940, on March 30. They remained married for sixty-five years, until her death on March 16, 2005. Three children were the products of their union: Nancy, Kathy, and Walter (Chip) III, married to actress Deborah Rush; and four grandchildren.

Both Walter Cronkite and Ed Bradley sought to convey the relevance of each news story and interviewee as influential subjects in the patchwork quilt of the unique individuality and the interwoven tapestry and 'fusion' of truth. Their stories covered and programs presented were educational. They shed new light on the biography, genealogy of the craft, of influential leaders, and legends that made and make a difference in the complex, yet fragile, fabric of our lives in all its bold, beautiful, audacious, innocence. In the midst of war, tension, and wrestling of the players on life's stage, presented in life-sized narratives that allowed the subjects to vicariously 'be in the moment' with no holds barred for, at least '60 minutes.'

With each journalist, we experienced valid, reliable journalism. Though the questions themselves may be replicated, the quality and unique character of the face-to-face exchanging and probing encounters yield historic etchings of permanence in the annals of time. Both men had strong beliefs firmly grounded by their faith in a power greater than themselves. We find it important in the recognition, and contribution made by their religious beliefs and practices to their individual spirituality, and formation of their unselfish character, sincere and genuine concern for others. Film, Liner Notes, and Spoken Word recordings were as important to Cronkite, as Jazz was to Bradley, whether he was in the audience as a spectator, or on the stage, 'jamming' with the musicians as an enthusiastic performer.

Philadelphia , Pennsylvania, the city of 'brotherly love and sisterly affection,' lays claim to and celebrates the sojourn of Ed Bradley as a 'favorite son,' beloved , along with the rest of the world, as an outstanding award-winning radio and television journalist and 'jazz man,' with a limited repertoire one song ('*Sixty—Minute Man)*, educator, humanitarian, mentor and role—model. New Orleans and Jazz Fest were second loves for Ed Bradley's alter-ego 'Teddy.'

Born Edward Rudolph Bradley, Jr. on June 22, 1941, to parents mother Gladys, and father Edward, as a child he was nicknamed 'Butch Bradley.' He was two years old when his parents divorced and his father moved to Detroit to work in the vending machine /restaurant business. His mother worked as a nurse and held a second job to make ends meet for she and her young son Ed. He was enrolled in an all-black Catholic boarding school, at age nine (9). the school was run by the Sisters of the Blessed Sacrament at Corn wells Heights, Pennsylvania. His continued educational endeavors, a combination of parochial and public, included attendance at Mount

Saint Charles Academy, located in Woonsocket, Rhode Island, and another historically black school, Cheyney University of Pennsylvania (formerly Cheyney State College). Ed Bradley was graduated from Cheyney in 1964 with a degree in Education. William B. Mann Elementary School in the Wynnefield community of Philadelphia was the site of his first teaching assignment. He taught sixth grade. Although teaching was his initial forte and first avocation, Ed soon discovered another compelling love, journalism. He spent time 'moonlighting' at radio station WDAS. Their studios were located in Fairmont Park, on Edgley Drive in Philadelphia. Initially volunteering to work for free and later for minimum wage, Bradley became a one person multi-tasking, staffer who covered basketball games, other sporting events, programmed music, and served as news reader.

His introduction to formal news reporting came in the 1960's when he covered the riots in Philadelphia for WDAS-FM. Subsequent to that work, in 1967, he was hired by CBS in New York for a radio station WCBS. He served in that capacity until 1971 when he decided to move to Paris, France, doing free-lance work and living off his savings, until his money ran out.

While in Europe at that time, he began working as a 'stringer' (part-time news correspondent) covering the Paris Peace Talks for CBS news. In 1972, he volunteered to transfer to Saigon to cover the Vietnam War, and spent time based in Phom Penh covering the war in Cambodia. It was there that he experienced a 'close-encounter of very personal kind with a mortar round while in a war-zone. While standing outside a complex, engaged in a conversation with a colleague, an unexpected mortar round landed in close proximity to where he was standing. The biographers note Ed Bradley's reflection following that event: "*That's when I hit the ground. So in the instant that that round landed and blew me in the air, I had those separate and distinct thoughts. The guy who was standing right next to where I had been standing had a hole in his back I could put by fist into.*" He received shrapnel wounds to his back and arm. Although he was flown back to France for recovery with the option to return to the United States, Bradley chose to return to Southeast Asia as the war drew to a close to complete the assignment he started there that was interrupted by his injury.

He moved to Washington, D.C. In 1974. He was promoted to covering the Carter campaign for President in 1976. This promotion by CBS news led to his enjoying the distinction of becoming the *first black White House television correspondent* for that network. *He was also the first black television correspondent to anchor his own news broadcast, CBS Sunday Night with Ed Bradley.* Ed Bradley was invited to move to *CBS Reports,* in 1978, to serve as the principal correspondent until 1981. In that same year Walter Cronkite left his position as anchor of the *CBS Evening News.* His replacement was Dan Rather, *60 Minutes* correspondent

Rather's departure from *60 Minutes* left the vacancy on the program that was filled by Ed Bradley who remained in that historical position for twenty-six years. During the course of that more than quarter century time frame, Bradley was privileged to cover over 500 stories, comprised of almost every type news genre possible. He covered segments on poverty, war, biographies, politics, sports, music, art, cuisine, screen, corruption, theater, national and international persons of note, and distinction. He began his career in broadcast journalism in the midst of the United States civil rights movement. Ed Bradley was the recipient of numerous awards for his outstanding work in performing his craft. Among the awards presented to him were the Pulitzer Prize, the Peabody Award, nineteen Emmy Awards which included one for '*Lena,*' *an interview with singer/actress Lena Horne; another for 'Made in China' an investigative piece on forced labor camps there; and 'In the Belly of the Beast' an interview with a convicted author/murderer.* He was also the recipient of the National Association of Black Journalists Lifetime Achievement Award and the Robert F. Kennedy grand prize in Journalism for his three hour documentary on violence in the United States, entitled '*In the Killing Fields of America.*'

Some of his most memorable media moments included conducting the first ever television interview in twenty years with singer Bob Dylan; playing blackjack with blind singer Ray Charles, conducting an interview in a sauna, with a Russian General; and one that we watched and experienced vicariously with Bradley, was the Lena Horne '*experience.*' It was quite evident to those of us in the viewing audience that Bradley was enthralled by the beautiful, legendary 64 year old singer. The then 42 year old correspondent appeared 'professionally awe struck' yet maintained his legendary journalistic style and grace. He later said of that interview: "*If I arrived at the Pearly gates and Saint Peter said, 'What have you done to deserve entry?' I'd just say, 'Did you see my Lena Horne story??*"

It seems both ironic and coincidental that the song most frequently performed by twenty six year CBS '60 Minutes' news man, 'Journalist-Jazz mans ' Ed—Teddy, was entitled *60 Minute Man*. This song, which became a rhythm and blues classic, was first popularized in 1951, by the singing group Billy Ward and the Dominoes. Audiences indicated enjoyment at hearing and seeing Bradley perform 'Sixty Minute Man.' Though he admitted his limited musicality he was a big fan and as often as his schedule would permit, performed on stage, with enthusiasm, with singer Jimmy Buffet and the Neville Brothers (Bradley was known by some people as the 'fifth Neville brother.')

Jazz trumpet player Wynton Marsalis was a lifetime friend of Ed Bradley's. Immersing himself into the role of Teddy, seem to serve as a 'catharsis' for the hard-working, often intense, journalist of excellence, Bradley. His numerous hats worn during his eventful sojourn included those of human rights/civil rights advocate, activist, friend, and mentor to journalists who included Charlene Hunter Gault and Gwen Ifill. Other African-American contemporaries included journalist Bernard Shaw of CNN and Max Robinson of ABC News. In memoriam, Bradley has been acclaimed as being a priceless 'gem' of a human being.

In memoriam to Cronkite's parallel broadcast journalist, Edward Rudolph Bradley, Jr. ('Ed' AKA 'Butch' and 'Teddy') who gasped his last breath with expressed concern for his wife and the dreams that he had so desperately wanted to share with her. As the cancerous contamination of leukemia coursed through his circulatory system, winning the race against, and blocking out the life sustaining oxygen supply, impeding its entry into his airways and the intricate pathways of capillaries, veins, arteries and lymph nodes; the cancer, with debilitating antagonism, eventually snuffed out his valiant life. Along with his beloved wife Patricia Blanchet, Charlayne Hunter-Gault and Jimmy Buffet were at Bradley's bedside when he transitioned from this life on November 9, 2006. In the death of one journalist, as in the life and deeds of both, these two pioneer sojourners of truth and justice, advocates for excellence and style in journalism, will be remembered for their magnanimity, and for the contributions they modeled with dignity, as stellar practitioners of the 'fourth estate.'

Quotations

Family lessons: " . . . I know that it is within families that we learn both the need to respect individual human dignity and to work together for our common good. Within our families, within our nation, it is the same. "

Ann Richards

On the subject of women in politics: "Ginger Rogers did everything Fred Astaire did. She just did it backwards and in high heels. "

Ann Richards

After cracking a half-century male grip on the governor's mansion at the state Capitol in Austin, Texas:

"A woman's place is in the dome. "

Ann Richards

In her 1991 Inaugural Address: "Today we have a vision of Texas where opportunity knows no race, no gender, no color-a glimpse of what can happen in government if we simply open the doors and let the people in."

Ann Richards

"Earlier today we heard the beginning of the Preamble to the Constitution of the United States, "We the people." It is a very eloquent beginning. But when that document was completed, on the seventeenth of September in 1787, I was not included in that "We, the people." I felt somehow for many years that George Washington and Alexander Hamilton just left me out by mistake. But through the process of amendment, interpretation, and court decision, I have finally been included in "We, the people."

Barbara Jordan

"What the people want is very simple-they want an America as good as its promise."

Barbara Jordan

"One thing is clear to me: We, as human beings, must be willing to accept people who are different from ourselves."

Barbara Jordan

"Think what a better world it would be if we all, the whole world, had cookies and milk about three o'clock every afternoon and then lay down on our blankets for a nap."

Barbara Jordan

CHAPTER 4

ANN RICHARDS

SEPTEMBER 1, 1933-SEPTEMBER 13, 2006

BARBARA JORDAN

FEBRUARY 21, 1936-JANUARY 17, 1996

Parallel voices and Proponents of Truth, Political Equity, Public Service and Justice

Dorothy Ann Willis Richards and Barbara Charline Johnson converged in their parallel life sojourns as American politicians from Texas. Their untiring efforts against injustice and unethical practices, especially in public service, were lifelong passions. Recognized for their integrity and dignity, both women displayed powerful, dedicated, compassionate, spirited, humility in all their endeavors. .Ann Richards's initial profession was that of Teacher. Barbara Jordan is noted as Attorney, and politician, who later became a teacher. President Lyndon B. Johnson was a political mentor to Barbara Jordan. Barbara Jordan in turn became a mentor to Ann Richards. She volunteered as an Ethics advisor to Richards. She also assisted her with interpreting legal precedents and constitutional law. Both women were longtime champions of minorities and women in government. They were advocates of empowerment of women and the underserved. They sought and shattered a number of political glass ceilings. Both enjoy the distinction of being *first In* a number of significant and prominent areas. Gifted debaters, both women spoke with eloquence and relevance. One editor wrote in a personal introduction to a book of Barbara Jordan speeches: *"Speaking the Truth with Eloquent Thunder." That she 'symbolized' the true meaning and essence of ethics and values.* In an interview given shortly before her death Jordan said: *"Ethical behavior means being honest, telling the truth, and doing what you said you would do."(Max Sherman, 2007) Jordan is recognized as one of the premier orators of the twentieth century.*

Ann Richards is remembered for her vitality, her beaming smile, her wit, sense of humor, big heart and big hair. Richards opened government in Texas to everyone. As governor she is noted for appointing the first black University of Texas regent, the first crime victim on to the state Criminal Justice board, the first teacher to lead the state Board of Education, the first disabled person on the human rights board and pinned stars on the first female and first black officers in the Texas Rangers. Assisted the first black, Ron Kirk in becoming mayor of Dallas, obtaining his first political internship during a state constitutional convention and subsequently appointed him to secretary of state. She is credited with bringing more women and minorities into power.

Historians tell us that Jordan devoted her life to reaching for and attaining goals that seemed unattainable, dreams that seemed impossible, and stars that seemed unreachable.

Notable 'Firsts' for Barbara Jordan include the following:

-First black to hold a major county administrative position-Named by Harris County Judge Bill Elliott as his administrative assist for welfare issues, 1965

-First African-American female to be elected to the Texas Senate, 1966

-First African-American elected Governor anywhere in the country in 1972—when she was elected to preside over a legislative body and to serve as president pro-temp ore of the Texas Senate.

-First African-American woman to represent Texas in Congress

-First African American woman to represent a previously Confederate state in Congress, 1972

-First African—American woman to deliver a keynote address at a political
   Convention, 1976

-First African—American woman to be buried at the Texas State Cemetery 1996, (an honor reserved for Texas heroes)

Ann Richards in her own right may be considered a 'hero' or better still a 'she-roe.' She was born on September 1, 1933, in Lakeview, Texas. Her parents were Mildred Iona Warren and Robert Cecil Willis. She was an only child. Because of her charm, wit, homespun sassy style, and pioneering spirit, Ann Richards was once described by a Texas newspaper as "*the quintessential Texas woman.*"

She and Barbara Jordan enjoyed a longtime relationship as friends, colleagues, mentor/mentee and uncompromising voices for truth and justice in public service regardless of the level. A strong and skillful debater, while attending Waco High School, in 1950, Ann Richards earned a college scholarship in debate, to Baylor University. After earning a bachelor's degree from Baylor, she was married to her high school sweetheart, David Richards (Dave). When they relocated to Austin, she attended the University of Texas, at Austin. She was graduated in 1955 after obtaining her teaching certificate.

Four children were the product of their marital union: Cecile, Daniel, Clark, and Ellen. Ann's grueling schedule related to her political activities, commitments and personal challenges soon took its toll and put a strain on her marriage to Dave. They ended the marriage in1980. About the same time she entered and completed a rehabilitation program for drinking which had become a pronounced problem.

Political work seemed to come naturally to Ann Richards whose tireless efforts resulted in two women Sarah Weddington (a lawyer who argued the winning side of Roe v Wade in from to the United States Supreme Court) and Wilhelmina Delco being elected to the Texas Legislature. *Her accomplishments also included presenting training sessions on campaign techniques for women candidates and managers statewide.* She presented the amendment to the delegates of the National Women's Conference, held in Houston in 1978, for the ratification of the Equal Rights Amendment to the Constitution. To date this issue is still pending since enough states have still not ratified the amendment for addendum to the Constitution.

Serving as a volunteer for several gubernatorial campaigns in 1950, marks the entrance of Ann Richards into the political arena. A capable campaign organizer, she ran the successful election campaign that resulted in the aforementioned Sarah Weddington being elected to the Texas legislature. In 1976 she waged her own first bid for public office. She successfully won the position as commissioner for Travis County. Moving from local to state government, in 1982 she won the election to State Treasurer, with this election she became the first woman elected to statewide office in more than fifty years. She was re-elected without opposition, to the post of treasurer, in 1986.

Richards was a popular, innovative and proactive, public servant. As State Treasurer she worked to maximize the return of Texas state investments. She observed that when she took office, the department was run like an antiquated country bank of the 1930's, housing deposits that did not earn interest. Her accomplishments as state treasurer positioned her into national prominence. As her political profile continued to rise, Richards was thrust into the national spotlight and invited to deliver the keynote address at the 1988 National Democratic Convention. Poignant remarks made by Richards during that rhetorically historic speech were:

> "When we pay billions for planes that won't fly, billions for tanks that won't fire, and billions for systems that won't work, that old dog won't hunt. And you don't have to be from Waco to know that when the Pentagon makes crooks rich and doesn't make America strong, it's a bum deal."

In 1990, was successful in her run for governor, serving from 1991-1995. She was the 39th Democratic governor to serve and considered by some historians to be the first woman elected governor, in her own right. Others document her as the second female because Miriam "Ma" Ferguson served as governor as a proxy after her husband James E. "Pa" Ferguson was impeached as governor.

Ann Richards made good on her campaign promises, pledging to add minorities and women to state government in her plan for a 'New" Texas She also created the state lottery system, implemented as a means to supplement school finances. She purchased the first lottery ticket on May 29, 1992, at Polk's Feed Store, in Oak Hill, a city located near Austin.

The slumping Texas economy was given a 'boost' and significantly revitalized under Richards's leadership. She attempted to streamline the states corporate infrastructure, government and regulatory institutions for business and the public. Her audits on the state bureaucracy saved six billion dollars in preparation for the expansive growth in the state which occurred later in the decade The prison system was improved by her reforms which served to reduce the number of violent offenders being released, and increased the prison space to cope with the growing prison population. Within the state she supported proposals to reduce the sale of semi-automatic firearms and so called "cop-killer" bullets. She also expended great effort to make the funding for schools more equitable across school districts. She also implemented "site-based management" in an effort to decentralize education policy control over individual campuses, and school districts.

Governor Richards enjoyed many milestones involving the Texas film and music industry, related to her longtime personal interest in these areas and her desire to raise public awareness in high profile locales within the state. as key to future economic growth plans for Texas. One of her first legislative requests was to move the Texas Film Commission and Texas Music Office out of the Department of Commerce and into the Governor's Office where it remains to this day. She put the spotlight on and gave legitimacy to film in Texas as a genuine industry. She was also influential in publishing the first Texas Music Industry Directory, 1991 and her "Welcome to Texas" speech to attendees on opening day of a South by Southwest Music and Media Conference, 1993. She was emcee every year for the Texas Film Hall of Fame. Her inability to perform that task in 2006 was due to her health challenges with cancer.

One true story that Ann Richards enjoyed sharing had to do with her friend Barbara Jordan. Apparently Jordan called her one day to request any assistance that she could provide to her in obtaining the appropriate zoning permit with the required authorization so that she could have a paved road constructed, thereby making her sprawling, and remote, suburban property more accessible to her visitors. One of her neighbors, an elderly woman, for reasons unknown to Jordan attempted to block her efforts to have the road built. In time, however, due in large part to Ann Richards's efforts expended on Jordan's behalf, the permit was obtained, and the road was built. Sometime later, after that incident, Ann asked Barbara: "Whatever happened to that woman who caused you so much grief about zoning for the road you built?" Barbara replied: "Oh, that old woman? She died and went to hell!!!" On that note they both enjoyed a good belly-laugh, to the point of tears. This is a prime example of traits that the two women had in common—candor, wit and humor with precise timing and delivery.

Barbara Jordan was sometimes referred to as a modern day Sojourner Truth. She was however, much more than the embodiment of that great woman. She was her own person deserving recognition for her own commanding presence and outstanding accomplishments. It's true that she was a legacy of greatness but she was also as an innovator, a trend setter, an emancipated, educated, sophisticated, *spellbinding orator of eloquence and an agent of positive change and progress* in her own right.

Barbara Jordan was born and raised in Houston, Texas (February 21, 1936), in an area known as the Fifth Ward, a predominantly black district. Her father, Benjamin Jordan was a part time Baptist minister, warehouse laborer. Her mother, Arlyn (Patten) Jordan, home maker, church activist, past church orator. Her up-bringing was very strict and most of the family activities were focused around the Good Hope Baptist Church. Barbara was the youngest of three children, all daughters, born to the Jordan's. Because she felt constrained by the family focus on the church, Barbara spent most of her time with her maternal grandfather, John Ed Patten. He was a former minister who had been imprisoned for shooting a white police officer, in self defense. After his release from prison he became an independent junk dealer. Barbara admired him for his courage and each Sunday she would assist him in sorting his rags and scrap iron, and would ride with him, around Houston, in his mule drawn wagon, to assist him in selling his junk to local merchants. They were each the others biggest supporter and source of encouragement. Her grandfather always encouraged her to follow her heart's desire regarding her life goals and career choice. At an early age she had expressed her desire to become a lawyer. Her choice of law as a career was based in her desire to seriously impact on racial injustice.

She attended Roberson Elementary and Phyllis Wheatley High School. While in high school, Jordan excelled in debating and won local, state, and national honors in debate. Consequently, she was the very deserving recipient of the National Usher's Oratorical Award. She was also inducted into the National Honor

Society. And was graduated in the upper five percent of her class in 1952. Her desire was to study political science at the University of Texas—Austin, but segregation made that a non-viable option at the time. Thus, she enrolled in an all-black college Texas Southern University (TSU) with a double major in political science and history. She was graduated magna cum laude in 1956. She pledged Delta Sigma Theta Sorority, a public service national and international organization of note, while enrolled at TSU. Although TSU was not her first choice, while there Barbara Jordan was encouraged by having the opportunity to fine-tune her debating and oratorical skills to the point of becoming, a national champion debater, under the tutelage of her debate coach, Mr. Tom Freeman.

The school traveling debate team consisted of all males. The coach had a firm policy of not allowing females to travel with the team. Barbara, however, was able to convince Mr. Freeman to allow her to participate with the traveling team based on her strength as a debater and skills as an orator. Prior to this point, because of segregation in public institutions, black debaters had been excluded from white debate contests. The Supreme Court decision to end segregation in public schools opened doors for the team that had previously been closed. Consequently, the 1954 decision regarding Brown vs. Board of Education was a very pivotal time for Barbara and her team mates. The Brown v Board decision provided opportunities which afforded the TSU team to debate and defeat opponents from such schools as Yale and Brown. Barbara Jordan was one of the first African Americans to accomplish still another notable feat when her team tied Harvard University in team debate.

Although Harvard's law school was her first choice, Barbara Jordan was discouraged from attempting to enroll after being advised that she would probably not be accepted because she was a black female from a Southern black university. Subsequently she attended law school at Boston University and upon graduation, successfully completed the bar exams and was admitted to the Massachusetts and Texas bars in 1959. It was at that time too, reflecting on her experience at Boston University, she made the observation that *separate* black and white schools were *not equal.* She noted that the black experience felt like years of remediation. The separation between the two systems was a serious detriment to the quality of education presented to the students and was in fact, not the same. Before returning to Houston to take the bar examination in 1960, and to practice law, Barbara Jordan, Esquire taught political science in an under-graduate degree program at Tuskegee Institute, in Alabama.

Upon her return to Houston, Barbara Jordan set up her first law practice within her family home. In 1962 and 1964 her attempts at being elected to the Texas House of Representatives were unsuccessful both times. In 1966 she made history by becoming the first African American since Reconstruction (1883) to be seated in the Texas Senate. This feat was due in no small part to a Supreme Court decision, resulting in redistricting to enforced "one person, one vote" as law. Becoming the first Black woman in the Texas legislature caused her to appear as somewhat of an oddity. She was also subject to a frigid environment, coupled with rude comments made by some of her male colleagues. In an interview with Molly Ivins, of the Fort Worth Star-Telegram, Lehrer News Hour, PBS Journalist, Charlayne Hunter-Gault, was told that Barbara Jordan coped admirably, endured with dignity, ignoring the ignorance of those hurling insults towards her, on a routine basis. (Barbara Jordan (2005) *http://nedv.net/community/blackhx/women/barbarajordan.php*) I read somewhere that regardless to what one is called, it's what one answers to that really matters. Jordan was reelected to the Senate in 1968.

In 1972, Barbara Jordan became a United States Congressperson after defeating Republican Paul Merritt to represent Texas' Eighteenth District in the House of Representatives. She thus became the first black woman elected to Congress from the South and along with Andrew Young of Georgia, one of the first two blacks elected to the U.S. Congress, since Reconstruction, from the South. Failing health presented her with challenges from multiple sclerosis and leukemia. Her ultimate decline due to both battling these debilitating diseases caused her to retire from politics in 1979. During her limited time serving as a state senator and U.S. Congressperson, Jordan was able to effectively fulfill her promise to champion the cause of the impoverished, downtrodden, minorities, disabled, and underrepresented, and those who were victims of injustice. As Texas State Senator, Jordan's work on the Worker's Compensation Act resulted in increasing to the maximum, the benefits paid to qualified injured workers. While in congress, she sponsored legislation to broaden the Voting Rights Act of 1965, to cover Mexican Americans in Texas and other southwestern states. This Act also extended the authority to those states in which minorities had been denied their voting rights or had their rights restricted by unjust, registration practices, such as literacy tests. She was a strong proponent and supporter of the Equal Rights Amendment as well.

She accepted a position at the University of Texas-Austin and became a professor, teaching intergovernmental relations, ethics, and political values. In 1994 she served on the U. S. Commission on Immigration Reform and served as ethics/advisor consultant to Governor Ann Richards during her term in office. She was very close to President Lyndon B. Johnson, who was her political mentor. She also became a Professor of Public Affairs at the Lyndon Baines Johnson School of Public Affairs.

The national prominence she gained for her work on the Watergate panel and her position taken in her riveting testimony, which captivated listeners and inspired many Americans to look more closely at the foundation and strength of our United States Constitution. The world took notice of Barbara Jordan and we believe that this global focus, led to her being selected to present a keynote speech at the Democratic National Convention, in 1976 and again in 1992. She made history in 1976 for being chosen to present the keynote address because the invitation made her the *first black woman selected to keynote a major political convention.* Many thought that because her speech was so memorable and presented with such power and 'eloquent thunder,' that Jordan would be considered as a vice presidential nominee and later as a possible Supreme Court Justice. She was certainly qualified to fill either role, however her aforementioned health issues limited those options being viable for her to pursue if presented to her for consideration. She was also considered by President Jimmy Carter for attorney general and United Nations Ambassador. But at that time she chose to remain in Congress.

Complications from pneumonia finally claimed her life on January 17, 1996. She was eulogized by President Bill Clinton, who among other accolades praised her work on the Clinton panel on Immigration Reform. In 1994 she was awarded the Presidential Medal of Freedom. Former Texas Governor, Ann Richards, joined President Clinton in eulogizing Barbara Jordan, her friend, advisor and mentor.

It seems impossible to mention the name Barbara Jordan, without consideration being given to a myriad adjectives connoting power worth emulating and presence to describe, accompany, and surround that name. Larger than life too are the statues erected in her honor, in Texas. One of these mammoth constructs is located at the University of Texas at Austin where Jordan taught until the time of her death. The Barbara Jordan Memorial statue was unveiled on April 24, 2009. It depicts her standing tall, with the right leg firmly planted, slightly ahead of the left leg. She appears balanced well grounded and unwavering in her look and stance. Her traditional hair style and facial features are very complimentary. She is well dressed in a professional business suit with the jacket open slightly. Her sleeves are pushed up both arms, a short distance, to free her hands and so as not to interfere with her apparent readiness to take on whatever task befalls her. Her facial features display a quiet confidence. Both hands are on her hips conveying to this writer—quiet strength, authority, boldness, maybe even defiance and perhaps a challenge to anyone that: "If you think you can take me on, . . . come on!" (Authors comment) We're told by the researchers that a combination of Jordan quotes are imprinted along with the statue to provide the viewer with insight as they read her thoughts and view the sculpture simultaneously. The overall essence is intended to depict her insatiable appetite for the *truth*.

The second statue is a likeness of Barbara Jordan in a seated position. This larger than life-size eight foot tall piece of sculpture, is a landmark for the Barbara Jordan Passenger Terminal at Austin—Bergstrom Airport, in Texas. The statue was unveiled in November, 2002 and is located in the main terminal, lower level of the four levels Barbara Jordan Passenger Terminal. The area surrounding the statue is open, airy, with steel supported glass windows and overlays. The sculpture depicts Jordan seated comfortably in a huge, draped, armchair. Her expression appears to be calm, compassionate and pensive. Her hands are peaked and touching in the classic pyramid which represents authority, power, control, and a contemplative posture. She is positioned to both greet and welcome travelers as well as to bid them goodbye as they move through the sunny, open Market Place, to baggage, and parking within an easy walking distance. Since Austin is not a hub and more of a destination airport, the design lends itself to making travel to and from Austin, pleasurable, memorable and a convenient experience.

Hope for justice, harmony, ethical leadership, along with racial and gender equality was a lifetime mission for Barbara Jordan. Each one of the memorials erected as a tribute to Jordan, symbolize the power and dynamism of her image in lasting, carefully detailed constructs of concrete, granite, steel and marble. In the airport and at the university, the statues are commanding replicas and lasting imprints of a woman who had the ability to simplify and clarify complex issues of the season in which she celebrated her sojourn here.

EPILOGUE

I awakened at sunrise on Independence Day morning, 2009 (July 4) and called upon Sojourner, Susan B., Eleanor, Mary, Ed, Walter, Ann and Barbara. They were summoned at this early hour, because their help was needed by this author, at that moment in time. I called upon them across the annals of time, to the table of their universality, to help me summarize just what it is that sets them apart as parallels in their life journey from the throngs of single notable individuals who have made significant contributions to history, her-story, human rights, civil rights, the arts, literature, etc. As I navigated through the complexities of their responses, they converged upon my mind's eye like a collage. Their voices were harmonious in their unity and balance, yet unintelligible in their diversity. I wanted to know why each one of them individually and collectively made such a profound difference and impact on this life journey. I asked them: "How can we best convey the universal application celebrating your synergy? After channeling these voices of truth and justice, I finally received the following *responses*, with clarity. I then proceeded to document as scribe (amanuensis) that which they had imparted to me to internalize:

First-We were all *flawed*. In the very act of living our humanity we were *imperfect beings, yet motivated by fierce and audacious hope.*

Second-We had *panoramic vision*. The '*big*' picture was always more appealing and challenging to us and required greater effort than the narrow tunnel view perspective.

Third-When we *came to a cross-road,* because of our gender, race, religion, geography, education, socio-economic status, injustice encountered, cultural biases and taboos, we each chose to take the *road less traveled.* That we believe is what has made the difference.

Fourth—We chose to *operate outside of the proverbial box, with an ultimate goal, purpose and direction set before us.* We then developed action plans and strategies to *achieve and attain seeming ordinary goals in an extraordinary manner.*

Fifth—We were sustained and maintained by our faith and belief in the ultimate and absolute power of our prime—mover. We were convinced that 'no-thing' is impossible. When you reach higher than what you think possible, what you can attain will transcend, exceed and become far greater than anything you could ever imagine.

Sixth—Even in the midst of global warfare, mental combat zones, economic chaos, financial collapse; crumbling, disintegrating moral ethical fiber, spiritual stagnancy, a need for a new awakening; societal dysfunction, high crime rates, urban blight, blatant injustice, political dishonesty, and bureaucratic imbalances; we *continued to move forward with determination, unwavering in the roles and tasks that life had designed for each one of us, individually and as parallels to the collective others. Ours was a philosophy of love, trust, compassion, justice, truth and confluence, within the unity, we sought.*

Seventh—We deemed it imperative to reach out, reach down, reach over, to reach behind to help and give aid to others in achieving their life given purpose, mission, and passion.

Eighth—We chose to celebrate each new day as a dynamic new beginning and new opportunity for being vehicles of change. We chose to seek becoming even better examples of humanity and agents to facilitate positive nurturing change in ourselves; without erecting barriers for others or constructing road-blocks to their progress, discovery and quest for the improbable vision in the near and distant future.

> *"Without a vision, the people perish. If it lingers wait for*
> *it will surely come."*
> *Habakkuk 2: 2-3*

REFERENCES

Susan B. Anthony. (Santa Rosa, CA: The National Women's History Project, 1994)

"Susan Brownell Anthony." *Women in History. Women in History: Living Vignettes of Women From the Past. 21 March 2006*

Cronkite, Walter. *Autobiography: A Reporter's Life.* (New York: Alfred A. Knopf, 1996)

Cronkite, Walter. "Free the Air Waves!" (*CBS News: 4 November 2002*)

Baker, Jean H. *Sisters: The Lives of America's Suffragists.* (New York: Hill and Wang, 2005) ISBN 0-8090-9528-9.

Banner, Lois W. *Elizabeth Cady Stanton A Radical for Women's Rights.* (Boston: Little, Brown & Company Limited, 1980)

Beasley, Maurine H., The *Eleanor Roosevelt Encyclopedia (2001)* online version

"Mary McLeod Bethune." *Gale Encyclopedia of U.S. Economic History. (Detroit:* Gale Research Group, 1999)

Bethune, Mary McLeod. *Mary McLeod Bethune Building a Better World Essays and Selected Documents.* ed. Audrey Thomas McClusky and Elaine M. Smith. (Indiana University Press, 1999)

Ed Bradley. *Wikipedia, the free encyclopedia (Biography, 2006)*

Bullock, Ralph W. "Mary McLeod Bethune" in *In Spite of Handicaps* (Freeport, N.Y.: Books for Libraries Press, 1968), 103-109

Carter, Polly. *Harriet Tubman and Black History Month.* (New Jersey: Silver Press, 1990)

Clardy, Andrea F. *Women's History Curriculum Guide.* (Santa Rosa, CA: The National Women's History Project, 1986)

Cooney, Barbara. *Eleanor.* (New York: Viking, 1996)

Clay, Augustella. 'Does it Make a Difference?' *The Spirit of Beauty . . . He Holds the Reins.* (Pennsylvania: Dorrance, 1995) 6

Edwards, Roanne. "Jordan, Barbara Charline." *Africana the Encyclopedia of the African American Experience.* ed. Kwame Anthony Appiah and Henry Louis Gates, Jr. (New York: Basic Civitas Books, 1999) 1067

Fay, Robert. "Bradley, Edward R."*Africana The Encyclopedia of the African and African American Experience.* ed. Kwame Anthony Appiah and Henry Louis Gates, Jr. (New York: Basic Civitas Books, 1999) 298-299

Fleming, Sheila Y. "Bethune – Cookman College." in *Black Women in America: An Historical Encyclopedia* (Brooklyn, N.Y.: Carlton Publishing Co., 1982) 127-128

Hearon, Shelby. *Barbara Jordan: A Self-Portrait.*(Garden City, New York: Doubleday, 1979)

Hitti, Miranda. "CBS'Ed Bradley Dies of Leukemia," (*CBS News, 2006*)

Holt, Rackham. *Mary McLeod Bethune: A Biography.*(Garden City, New York: Doubleday and Co., Inc., 1964)

Keough, Leyla. "Bethune, Mary McLeod." *Africana the Encyclopedia of the African American Experience,* ed. Kwame Anthony Appiah and Henry Louis Gates, Jr. (New York: Civitas Books, 1999) 229-230

Lash, Joseph. *Eleanor and Franklin.* (New York: W.W. Norton, 1971)

Lash, Joseph. *Eleanor: The Years Alone* (New York: W.W. Norton, 1972)

Linder, Sarah. "Richards was a Friend of Texas Film. *Austin American Statesman* (Austin ,Texas: web:AR,2006)

Linder, Douglas. Famous American Trials: The Anthony Trial: An Account *Argument for the Defense Concerning Legal Issues in the Case of: United States vs. Susan B. Anthony. (2001)*

Love, Dorothy M. ed. "Mary Jane McLeod Bethune" in *A Salute to Historic Black Women*(Chicago: Empak Publishing Co., 1984) 6

Mabee, Carlton with Susan Mabee Newhouse. *Sojourner Truth: Slave, Prophet, Legend* (New York and London: New York University Press, 1993)

The National Council of Negro Women, Inc. *The Black Family Reunion Cookbook.* (Tennessee: The Wimmer Companies, 1991)

Parham, Sandra. ed. *Barbara C. Jordan-Selected Speeches.* (Washington, D.C.: Howard University Press, 1999

Painter, Nell Irvin. S*ojourner Truth: A Life, A Symbol* (New York and London: W.W. Norton & Co., 1996)

Patriot Ledger Staff. *Role Model: Susan B. Anthony to come to life.* (Quincy , MA: The Patriot Ledger: City Edition, 1 March 2006)

Raines, John C. *The Justice Men Owe Women.* (Minneapolis: Fortress Press, 2001)

Reagon, Bernice. "Bethune, Mary Jane McLeod" in *Dictionary of American Negro Biography* (New York: W.W. Norton and Co., 1982) 41-43

Richards, Ann. Richard U. Levine, M.D. *I'm Not Slowing Down; Winning My Battle With Osteoporosis.* (Texas: Plume, 2004)

Richards, Ann. Knobler, Peter. *Straight from the Heart: My Life in Politics and Other Places.* (New York: Simon & Schuster, 1989)

Rogers, Mary Beth. *Barbara Jordan: American Hero.* (New York: Bantam Doubleday Dell Pub., 1998)

Roosevelt, Eleanor. *The Autobiography of Eleanor Roosevelt.* (New York: Da Capo Press ed., 1992)

Schorn, Daniel. "The Personal Side of Ed Bradley. (New York: CBS News, 2006-12-31)

Staff Writers. "Legendary '60 Minutes' Correspondent Ed Bradley Has Died." *ABC News. (2006-11-09)*

Teutsch, Austin. *Barbara Jordan: The Biography.* (Texas: Golden Touch Press, 1997)

Thomas, Betty Collier. "Sojourner Truth." *Daughters of Thunder.* (San Francisco: Jossey-Bass Publisher, 1998) 53-56